WITHDRAWN

Lake Villa Intermediate School
Lake Villa, Illinois 60046

D1622050

Lake Villa Intermediate School
Lake Villa, Illinois 60046

37500

TRUDY J. HANMER

NICARAGUA

A GROLIER COMPANY

Franklin Watts
New York/London/Sydney/Toronto/1986
A First Book

Map by Vantage Art, Inc.

Photographs courtesy of: Shostal Associates: p. 9;
New York Public Library Picture Collection: p. 28;
UPI/Bettmann Newsphotos: pp. 35, 40, 44, 49, 53 (bottom);
James Natchwey, Black Star: pp. 50, 53 (top), 60 (bottom);
Andrew Holbrooke, Black Star: p. 60 (top).

Library of Congress Cataloging in Publication Data

Hanmer, Trudy J.
Nicaragua.
(A First book)
Includes index.
Summary: Surveys the people, customs, climate,
culture, traditions, and turbulent history of the
largest country in Central America.
1. Nicaragua—Juvenile literature. [1. Nicaragua]
I. Title.
F1523.2.H36   1986   972.85   85-26348
ISBN 0-531-10125-8

Copyright © 1986 by Trudy J. Hanmer
All rights reserved
Printed in the United States of America
6   5   4   3   2   1

CONTENTS

NICARAGUA

For Rebecca and Benjamin

CHAPTER 1

A COUNTRY IN
THE NEWS

Nicaragua is a country in the headlines of major newspapers almost every day. This has not always been true, but for the past three hundred years, Nicaragua has time and again attracted the attention of the world. European nations have fought bitterly over the fate of this Central American country. So have the United States and many of Nicaragua's closest neighbors.

Although Nicaragua is the largest country in Central America, it is small in comparison to such world powers as China, the U.S.S.R., and the United States. And, although its land mass is significant by Central American standards, Nicaragua has fewer people per square mile than any of the other nations in Central America. Less than three million people live in the entire country.

Why has this tiny country created so much excitement? In large part the geography of Nicaragua has been responsible for its position at or near the center of world politics. From the time of Christopher Columbus's exploration of the New World,

Nicaragua's location has been the focus of many people's dreams and schemes. For Columbus, sailing in 1502 along the coast of what we now call Nicaragua, the dream was to find a passage to India, a land he believed to be rich in gold and spices. Later on, in the sixteenth and seventeenth centuries, other explorers thought Nicaragua was the one place where the two great oceans —the Atlantic and the Pacific—might be joined.

In modern times the idea of uniting two oceans continued to attract Americans and Europeans who believed that they could make their fortunes by digging a canal across Nicaragua. Such a canal would provide inexpensive and easier access to the west coast of the United States for Europeans and Americans living on the eastern coast of North America. Since the late nineteenth century, the government of the United States has been interested for strategic reasons in Nicaragua as well as other Latin American countries.

First, Nicaragua was believed to be important to the maintenance of United States naval power. Most recently, Nicaragua has been part of a struggle in which the United States as leader of the "Free World" nations has battled against the expansion of Communism in the Western Hemisphere. The United States has not been the only country to take an interest in Nicaragua. Since 1800 Great Britain, Germany, and Cuba, among others, have on occasion been concerned about their relationships with Nicaragua.

Nicaraguans have not always been pleased by all this outside interest in their nation. From the beginning of the Spanish exploration, foreign involvement in Nicaragua has often meant the violation of the rights of the people already living there, and this pattern has continued through every change of power in Nicaragua, including the most recent revolution. Too often foreigners have believed that they know what is right for Nicaragua. Also, groups within Nicaragua have seized power and then have brutally punished their opponents instead of working with them. As a result, Nicaragua is a poor country with a history of unstable governments.

At the same time, there are many things to make Nicaragua very proud of their country. It is a land of breathtaking beauty with high mountains that were created from volcanoes. The lakes of Nicaragua are among the largest and most unusual in Central America. Exotic animals and plants live in and around these lakes. Nicaraguans have a heritage that has combined the best of Spanish and Indian crafts and customs. Their weaving and jewelrymaking are famous all over the world.

As much as they love their nation, many Nicaraguans are worried right now about the fate of their country. They have been at war for many years, and peace seems increasingly hard to achieve. Nicaraguan families have been divided by the war, many of their homes have been destroyed, and much of the nation's business has been disrupted.

How, we might ask, has this small country become the site of so much turmoil? How did Nicaragua, a peaceful Indian nation in the 1400s, become the culturally mixed, politically turbulent nation that it is today? This book will help to answer these questions.

HONDURAS

Segovia River

NICARAGUA

● Chinandega

● Esteli

Lake Managua

Rio Grande de Matagalpa

● Leon

Managua ★

Masaya ●
Granada ●

OMETEPE
ISLAND

Escondido River

Bluefields ●

Lake Nicaragua

CARIBBEAN
SEA

PACIFIC
OCEAN

San Juan River

COSTA
RICA

NICARAGUA

CHAPTER 2

THE LAND AND
THE CLIMATE

Nicaragua is nestled among the seven countries that comprise the area of the world that we call Central America. The others are, from north to south, Guatemala, Belize, Honduras, El Salvador, Costa Rica, and Panama. Panama was originally part of Colombia, a country in the north of South America, and Belize used to be known as British Honduras. Belize is the one nation in Central America that has never had a dominant Spanish population. For these reasons, Nicaragua's ties have been historically closest to four of its neighbors—Guatemala, El Salvador, Honduras, and Costa Rica.

All of the Central American countries, including Nicaragua, are located on an isthmus that connects the southern part of North America to the northern part of South America. This isthmus runs between the two largest oceans in the world, the Atlantic and the Pacific, although technically the Caribbean Sea separates the land of Nicaragua from the body of the Atlantic Ocean. The Pacific coast of Nicaragua is 219 miles (350 km) long and the

Caribbean coast is 336 miles (537 km) long. All together, Mexico, the nations of Central America, and the nations of South America are called Latin America, a name that reflects the Spanish influence in these lands. Spanish is a language derived from Latin, and Spanish is the official language of almost all the nations of Latin America, including Nicaragua.

Volcanoes and Mountains

The isthmus on which Nicaragua and the other Central American countries are located was probably formed over a long period of time by the activity of volcanoes. There are still many active volcanoes in Nicaragua, and the most important mountain ranges in the country are really chains of volcanoes. The mountain ranges cross the country from the northwest to the southeast. The two main ranges are the Cordillera de los Marabios, which runs close to the Pacific Ocean, and the Sierra de Amerrique. To the east of these two major chains of mountains are smaller mountain ranges, the Huapi, the Cordillera Dariense and the Cordillera Isabella. This last mountain range contains the highest peaks in Nicaragua.

The mountains of Nicaragua are important for several reasons. First, of course, they are distinctive and help make Nicaragua the beautiful country it is. More important, though, because they are really volcanoes, they are carefully watched by the Nicaraguans. Not only do the volcanoes occasionally erupt and shoot lava over the land, but they also create frequent earthquakes below the ground that have been very destructive to Nicaragua over the years. Finally, the volcanic mountains are partially responsible for the climate in Nicaragua.

Let us look first at the volcanoes and earthquakes that have been part of Nicaraguan life since the earliest recorded history.

In fact, the first known evidence of human life in Nicaragua is a set of fossilized footprints that archeologists believe to have been made by ancient people several thousand years ago who were fleeing from the hot lava of a volcanic eruption.

The highest volcano in Nicaragua is El Viejo (The Old One). Other important volcanoes are Mombacho, located near the city of Granada (it last erupted in 1560) and Cosequizina, which erupted so violently in 1835 that over half its height blew off in the explosion. Other smaller volcanoes now exist as islands in the middle of Nicaragua's lakes. An example of one of these is Ometepe, an island in the center of Lake Nicaragua. Ometepe is actually composed of two volcanoes, Concepción and Madera. At least eight small villages have been built on Ometepe, proof that the Nicaraguans have learned to coexist with the volcanoes that dominate the skyline.

Although most Nicaraguans probably do not think about the volcanoes every day, every once in a while violent earthquakes occur which show them that this special geographic feature of their country is not something to be ignored. Of the twenty major volcanoes in Nicaragua, eight are "active." This means that they have erupted in modern times and are likely to do so again. Volcanoes that have erupted in the 1980s include San Cristóbal, Concepción, Momotombo, and Telica.

Perhaps the most devastating destruction caused by volcanic action has occurred in Managua. This capital city of Nicaragua has been nearly destroyed twice in the twentieth century by earthquakes, once in 1931 and again in 1972. Managua is a city built on old volcanic rock that has been pressed together, rather than on the solid rock on which most other cities rest. Managua lies within a chain of volcanoes that has been called "a circle of fire" because these volcanoes are so apt to explode. This "chain of fire" includes volcanoes and fault lines—breaks in the earth that are susceptible to earthquakes—that extend from the Aleutian Islands in the northern Pacific all the way around to Japan and New Zealand. This ring passes through the American continent beneath Managua.

In 1972 the city found itself directly on the epicenter of an earthquake that occurred nine miles below the surface of the earth. As had happened in 1885 and in 1931, the tremors and explosions toppled buildings, disconnected water lines, disrupted fuel supplies, and killed many people. In the 1931 earthquake 1,450 citizens of Managua had died. In 1972, more than 8,000 people died and another 20,000 were seriously injured. The city has still not rebuilt completely from this worst recent natural disaster.

With earthquakes and volcanic explosions recurring in the same places, it seems strange that Nicaraguans do not move their capital city or their second largest city, Granada, also located near a volcano. The reason they do not is that there is a good side to living in this area of volcanic activity. The land here is extremely fertile because of the volcanic ash that has fallen on it. In fact this land is so choice that for as long as there have been records, three-quarters of all people inhabiting Nicaragua have lived in the area of the Pacific lowlands, even though it is sometimes dangerous. In this region, which runs from the Gulf of Fonseca in the northwest to the Costa Rican border, are located two of the largest and most beautiful lakes in Central America, Lake Managua and Lake Nicaragua. These lakes were formed by volcanic action.

Nicaragua's Lakes

Lake Nicaragua is especially interesting. At 3,000 square miles (7,770 sq km), it is the largest body of water between Canada

Lake Managua, against a backdrop of volcanic mountains,
provides a picturesque setting for an oil refinery.

and Lake Titicaca. Geographers believe that it was formed when an earthquake cut it off from the Pacific Ocean. One of the reasons they believe this is the presence in Lake Nicaragua of many varieties of saltwater fish that have adapted to life in this freshwater lake. Lake Nicaragua is the only freshwater lake in the world that contains tarpon, sharks, and swordfish, fish that normally live in salt water. Scientists theorize that these saltwater fish were trapped when Lake Nicaragua was cut off from the Pacific and that they adapted to living in fresh water as Lake Nicaragua changed character over the years from a salt- to a freshwater lake.

Although both Lake Nicaragua and Lake Managua are located on the Pacific coast of Nicaragua, they empty into the Caribbean by way of Nicaragua's most important river, the San Juan. The two lakes are connected by another important river, the Tipitapa. Other rivers that have long been vital to the Nicaraguan system of transportation include the Coco, the Viejo, the Amalia, the Punta Gorda, the Escondido, the Grandede Matagalpa and a host of smaller tributaries.

The Central Highland and the Miskito Coast

As important as the region of the Pacific lowlands is to an understanding of Nicaragua, there are two other distinct regions that cover three-quarters of the country. East of Managua is the region known as the central highland. This area is composed of rugged mountains, most of which are covered by a dense rain forest. The annual rainfall here varies between 70 and 100 inches (178 and 254 cm) which makes this area very uncomfortable for habitation. However, this area is home to the rich mining district known as Nueva Segovia. For generations people have been willing to submit to the humid climate in order to mine the silver and gold of the region.

As humid as the central highlands are by most North American standards, they are dry compared to the third geographic section of Nicaragua. This is the area known as "La Mosquitia" or the Miskito coast. (In translating this word first from the Indian and then from the Spanish, Miskito has come to be spelled a variety of ways in English: Miskito, Moskito, Mosquito.) However it is spelled, the word means the same thing—the eastern third of Nicaragua stretching along the Caribbean coast from Honduras in the north to Costa Rica in the south. "La Mosquitia" is the wettest area of all of Central America. Annual rainfall here averages from 100 to 250 inches (254 to 635 cm). The soil here is composed of gravel and sandy clay, and the only variation in the region comes in the vast area of savanna that covers the Mosquitia plain. Savanna is an area of treeless grassland.

Climate

Although the three areas of Nicaragua are very different in terms of the amount of rainfall they receive, one can say that overall Nicaragua is a tropical country with a tropical climate. The average temperature hovers in the 80s F. (high 20s C.) year-round, although in the mountain villages at the highest elevation the average temperature may be in the 60s F. (about 15° C.). The mountain ranges keep the western part of the country drier than the eastern half, but in all areas of Nicaragua there is a wet season and a dry season. The rainy season is called *invierno* and runs from May to January. The dry season is called *verano* and exists during the other months of the year. Invierno is interrupted by a few weeks in July and August when the weather is very hot and the rains stop altogether. This period of time each year is called *veranillo*.

Because of the great variety of land elevation in Nicaragua (distance above sea level), there are also several varieties of climate. Most people, however, live in areas where the pattern is one of invierno and verano. People who live in the mountains more than six thousand feet (1,830 m.) above sea level are said to live in the *tierra fría*, or cold land. Here temperatures are cooler and the air is very thin. People living at sea level live in the *tierra caliente*, or hot land. The ideal climate lies between 2,000 and 6,000 feet (610 and 1,830 m.) the *tierra templada*, where the temperatures are more moderate. Because so much of Nicaragua's good farmland lies near the lakes and seas, few people live at the higher, more comfortable elevation.

Because of the diversity of climate, there is a wide variety of plants and animals in Nicaragua. The vegetation in Nicaragua varies from trees and plants in the tropical rain forest to the kinds of trees and plants familiar throughout much of North America. In Nicaragua one can find cedar, oak, and pine trees as well as mahogany, ebony, persimmon, tamarind, indigo, coconut palm, and many other tropical plants.

The types of animals in Nicaragua are as numerous as the species of plants. Deer, rattlesnakes, and coyotes, familiar to North Americans, can be found, but so can tropical animals such as monkeys, puma, pelican, and toucan. Jaguars, wild boar, tapia, and sloths are not uncommon in the less populated areas of the country. The quetzal, a beautiful bird with a scarlet breast and bright green tail feathers, is now extinct, but used to live in the Nicaraguan forests.

Nicaragua's geography, its climate, its trees and its animals make it a land full of variety and surprises. Not surprisingly, the history of Nicaragua has been as colorful as the nation itself.

CHAPTER 3

NICARAGUA'S BEGINNINGS—
THE INDIANS
AND THE CONQUISTADORS

There is a strip of land between the Pacific Ocean and lakes Managua and Nicaragua that makes up its own separate isthmus. This area was the site of the first recorded meeting between people from North America and people from South America. It was here at the place that modern Nicaraguans call Rivas that mountain tribespeople who were part of the Aztec Empire first met the hill people from the southern area.

These Indians did not even speak the same language. The Northerners spoke a language called Nahua, and the Southerners spoke a language called Chibcha. Both groups, however, were part of the large group of "Amerindians" that were living in Central America long before the first Europeans explored this area.

When anthropologists speak of the Indian civilizations that inhabited Central America long ago, they speak of the Aztecs as having the "highest" form of civilization. By highest they mean that the Aztec form of government, economy, and religion were the most complex and the most modern that the Spanish encountered when they arrived in the New World.

However, as is true of any culture, it took many generations for the Aztecs to develop their civilization. Archeologists and anthropologists have studied ruins and fossils in Central America, and they believe that as early as 11,000 B.C. there were people living in Central America. These were Indians who possibly used the Central American isthmus as a footbridge between North and South America. Anthropologists refer to the areas of early Indian habitation as Mesoamerica. They divide Mesoamerica into three areas: southeastern Mesoamerica, central Mesoamerica, and lower Central America. Nicaragua is located in the last region.

Just as anthropologists divide Indian history geographically, they also divide it chronologically (by time period). Although many thousands of years of Indian history occurred before the Europeans came to the New World, all of the time before Spanish exploration is called pre-Columbian. This period covers many, many years, but since we have very little evidence to explain exactly what was happening to the Indians of Central America during those years, we group together large periods of their history.

Although there is evidence that people lived in many parts of Central America as early as 11,000 B.C., there is no sign that people lived in Nicaragua until about 5,000 B.C. At that time we know that farming Indians whose agriculture was based on corn, or maize, occupied the country that later came to be called Nicaragua. Some time between 300 B.C. and A.D. 300 these Indians moved from being cave dwellers to living in simple villages. At about this same time agriculture replaced hunting and fishing as the most important activities of the villagers.

The next stage in the development of these Central American Indian cultures occurred over the course of the following five hundred years. By A.D. 800 the Indians of lower Central America had developed art, particularly pottery, and their society was beginning to be stratified. Stratification means that different people, according to their skills, personalities, or jobs, were beginning to hold a variety of positions in the village society. Between 800 and 1500, the time of the coming of the Europeans, the process of stratification continued. Villages multiplied and began to establish trading networks with each other. Religion was very important, and the Indians created large stone statues as tributes to their gods.

The Nicarao Indians

In Nicaragua during this time, the culture of the Nicarao Indians was flourishing. Like other Central American Indians, the Nicarao were an argricultural people who lived in villages. As would be true of all people living in Nicaragua right up to the present day, the Nicarao chose to inhabit the Pacific lowland area because of its fertile soil. Besides maize, the Nicarao grew sweet potatoes. Cacao was another important product, and cacao beans were used as money.

The Nicarao were considered an advanced or high culture because of their sophisticated methods of farming, their types of dwelling, their cooking, and their trade. In all of this they resembled the Maya culture. Nicarao Indians lived in single family homes and made their maize into flour and then into a flat kind of bread we now call a tortilla.

To prepare their fields for planting, the Nicarao burned the brush and vines away from the soil. This process not only cleaned the land, but the ash temporarily fertilized the soil. To keep the soil good, they rested their fields every year or so. Modern farmers still use this process, called crop rotation. The Nicarao planted seeds individually by using sharp sticks to poke holes in the ground for the seeds. Another important aspect of their economy was their use of specialized markets. Farm products, pottery, cloth, and other goods were sold separately.

Some historians believe that the markets and trading of the Nicarao may have been stimulated by the great Aztec Empire to the north. Until the Spaniards destroyed the Aztecs in the 1500s, there was an Aztec trading colony located within the borders of present-day Nicaragua. It was believed by the Spaniards that the Aztecs used this colony to bring emeralds up to Mexico from somewhere in South America.

The Arrival of the Spaniards

Finding the source of these emeralds first attracted Spanish explorers to the "land of the Nicarao," which would soon become the Spanish colony of Nicaragua. The Spanish explorer Hernán Cortés had established a military government in Mexico by overthrowing the government of the Aztec Indians. Cortés wanted to find the source of the Aztecs' emeralds. About 1523 he sent one of his lieutenants, Pedro de Alvarado, known as the "conqueror of Guatemala," south to Nicaragua. Meanwhile, another Spanish conquistador, Pedrarias of Panama, sent one of his lieutenants, Hernández de Córdoba, to enter Nicaragua from the South. He was searching for the same gems. In this struggle the southerners were successful, and Córdoba became the first Spanish explorer of any importance in Nicaragua. He founded both León and Granada as Spanish colonial cities. Over the next three hundred years of Spanish rule, these two cities would become Spain's most important colonial outposts in Nicaragua.

Córdoba had dreams of making Nicaragua a separate Spanish province, and he rebelled against his leader in Panama. Because of this disloyalty, Pedrarias ordered Córdoba's head to be cut off.

Pedrarias then became governor of Nicaragua for a brief period of time, from 1526 to 1531.

By the time Pedrarias became governor of Nicaragua, the Spaniards had been exploring and colonizing Latin America since the early voyages of Christopher Columbus in the 1490s. Several European nations and individuals claimed to have "discovered" the New World earlier than Columbus, but it was his voyages that focused the attention of Europeans on the "new" continent. For this reason historians have long said that the official discovery of America, including Nicaragua, was made by Christopher Columbus in 1492. Of course, no European really discovered any part of America because the Indians knew it was there all the time.

Columbus's most famous voyage was his first one. However, he and his men, traveling aboard the *Niña*, the *Pinta*, and the *Santa María*, never reached the mainland of Central or South America on their first voyage. It was not until his fourth voyage, in 1502, that Columbus landed on the Central American mainland near Honduras. From there his party sailed south to Panama, stopping at various points along the way, including a place at the mouth of the San Juan River in Nicaragua.

All the lands that Columbus "discovered" he claimed for Spain. In 1493 and 1494 Spain and Portugal, another seagoing nation interested in foreign exploration, had made an agreement under the guidance of Pope Alexander VI that Spain could have all of the land west of a certain line of longitude in the Western Hemisphere, and Portugal could have all the discoveries to the east of this line. All of Central America lay to the west of the line. The official language of Nicaragua is Spanish today because of this decision. More important, Nicaragua was ruled by Spain for three hundred years because of this agreement, called the Line of Demarcation.

Other Spanish explorers followed Córdoba to the shores of Central America. Among them was Vasco Nuñez de Balboa who in 1513 crossed the isthmus and was probably the first European to see the Pacific Ocean. Men like Balboa were called *conquistadors*. After rumors spread through Spain in 1514 that great wealth could be found in Central America, many conquistadors sailed to America.

Early Spanish Settlements in Nicaragua

One of the largest expeditions was headed by Pedro Arias de Avila. He became Pedrarias, the man who controlled Panama at the time of the first land explorations into Nicaragua. When Pedrarias came to Panama, he made it clear to the Indians that they would live under Spanish laws and religion from then on. He read the Requerimento to the Central American natives. This document explained the Spanish version of the history of the world and the history of the Christian Church. Pedrarias told the Indians that they must accept Spanish rule and the Roman Catholic Church, the official religion of Spain. He hoped they would accept this peacefully, he told them, but if not, he would conquer them by force.

Pedrarias was typical of Spanish conquistadors. What happened in Panama happened elsewhere in Latin America, including Nicaragua. The conquistadors were determined to impose Spanish laws, customs, and religion on the Indians of Central America. Although many of the natives resisted, the Spaniards won.

It has been estimated that between 1519 and 1650, two-thirds of all Indians living in Central America lost their lives to the Spaniards through disease, warfare, and slavery. In addition to the Nicarao, two other Indian tribes, the Suma along the northern border of Nicaragua and the Miskito Indians along the Miskito coast, were badly hurt by the Spanish invaders.

Spanish Colonial Government

Although Central America became a part of the Spanish Empire in the New World, it was never as important to Spain as were other areas such as Mexico and Peru. The branch of the Spanish government that controlled the new properties in America was called the Supreme Council of the Indies. The highest office in the New World was that of viceroy, and the earliest viceroys were placed in Lima, Peru, and Mexico City. Christopher Columbus was an early viceroy; he and other viceroys who followed him chose to make their homes among the islands of the Caribbean. Wherever they lived, their power covered all of Central America and all the Spanish colonies in South America.

In addition to the viceroy, the Spaniards set up other governmental offices. In fact, they set up an elaborate system of government to control all aspects of the everyday life of the Spaniards and Indians in the colonies—their trade, their religion, their customs, and their laws. Central America was divided into three judicial (or court) areas, and these tended to be the center of all government power. Each judicial area was called an *audiencia*. Until 1570 the Audiencia of Santo Domingo controlled Nicaragua and Honduras on the mainland as well as many islands in the Caribbean.

Beginning in 1570 Nicaragua fell under a new audiencia, the Audiencia of Guatemala. This audiencia controlled all of Central America from Chiapas to Costa Rica for the next two hundred years. The chief administrator of the audiencia became the president, the governor, and the head of the military, all rolled into one. In this way the Spaniards in Latin America did not distinguish clearly among the executive, legislative, and judicial branches of government.

For Nicaraguans living under the Audiencia of Guatemala, the most important official was called the governor. He was always a man appointed by the Spanish king. In addition to the governor, the King of Spain appointed men called *alcaldes majores* who ruled over sizable Spanish settlements. The governor appointed men called *corregidors* who ruled the towns that were inhabited primarily by Indians. The corregidors were often cruel to the Indians under their control.

In the 1760s the Spanish introduced a new system of government in Central America. New local leaders, called *intendentes*, were installed in Chiapas, El Salvador, Honduras, Comayagua, and Nicaragua. At home in Spain the Spaniards were an urban people, used to living in towns and cities, and they carried this tradition to their American colonies. Each city had a *cabildo*, or town council. The town councilmen, called *regidores*, were originally chosen by the property owners. As time passed the office of regidore became hereditary and was passed from father to son among the landowners. The cabildos appointed local magistrates known as *alcaldes ordinarios*.

From the time of Pedrarias until the end of the 1700s, the Spanish in Central America lived pretty much as they chose. Although their chief leaders were appointed by the Spanish king, they were not that important to him and they were allowed to lead their own lives. As the eighteenth century grew to a close, however, the winds of change that sparked revolution in France and the United States swept through the nations of Latin America.

CHAPTER 4

INDEPENDENCE
COMES
TO NICARAGUA

During the years between Columbus's expedition and the re-organization of the Spanish colonial government under Charles III, King of Spain, a group of people called *criollos* had risen to a position of prominence in Nicaragua and other Latin American countries. Criollos were people of Spanish ancestry who were born in and lived in the Spanish colonies. By the 1800s they had gotten used to running their own government with little interference from the mother country.

Revolution Against
the Spanish King

The criollos's control was challenged by the changes under Charles III. Charles and his ministers in Spain tightened up the administration of the colonies. The criollos particularly resented the new restrictions on their trade. They felt that the *peninsulares* (Spaniards who lived overseas) should not make laws for them.

Then in 1808 the French dictator, Napoleon Bonaparte, invaded Spain and deposed the Spanish king, Ferdinand VII, who was the son of Charles III and had recently assumed the throne. The governor of Guatemala, a man named Antonio González Mollinedo y Saravia, had been appointed by Charles III and he worried that the criollos might take advantage of the French invasion to rebel against Spain. To prevent this, he restricted the freedom of the people of Guatemala. The French wrote a new constitution for Spain that encouraged greater freedom for the criollos. Under the terms of this document, the province of Guatemala got a greater measure of self-government and earned the right to elect twelve representatives to the Spanish legislature.

In 1811 Mollinedo was killed. He was succeeded by José de Bustamante y Guerra, an unpopular leader. Bustamante refused to allow the new rights that had been established by the constitution. His seven-year rule was marked by such repression that it has been called "el terror Bustamante." Revolts began to break out in cities throughout the province, first in Rivas and then in Granada and León. Each time Bustamante used troops to force the rebels into submission. Each time many people died, and the determination of the colonists to break free from Spain grew stronger. The situation did not change when the French were driven from Spain in 1814, and King Ferdinand VII was returned to power.

All over the world people were fighting for freedom, and the idea of liberty spread to Latin America. The United States had led the way by revolting from England in the American Revolution. France had followed the path of revolution and freedom when the peasants of that country overthrew King Louis XVI and his wife, Marie Antoinette. Great writers and thinkers like the French Jean Jacques Rousseau and Voltaire and the British John Locke and Mary Wollstonecraft urged new forms of freedom. The people of Latin America read and discussed these revolutionary ideas.

After almost three hundred years of living in Latin America, the criollos felt more like Latin Americans than they did like Spaniards. Some had never seen the land of their ancestors. The Latin American provinces were their countries, and they wanted to have full control over their governments. In their planning they forgot that the Indians had originally owned the land. The criollos had no intention of allowing the Indians to share in ruling Latin America once they gained their freedom from Spain.

The criollos of Guatemala declared their independence from Spain in 1821. The citizens of the Nicaraguan city of León then announced that they were splitting off from the rest of Guatemala. Granada, on the other hand, declared that it would remain with the original province. It was soon apparent that neither León nor the rest of the province was ready for complete independence. In 1822 both León and its rival city, Granada, voted to join Mexico. The union with Mexico lasted only one year. In 1823 Nicaragua agreed to join with Guatemala, El Salvador, Honduras, and Costa Rica. The five nations together called themselves the United Provinces of Central America.

Independence from Spain: the United Provinces

The United Provinces were organized under a constitution that provided for the election of a president every four years, the establishment of a bicameral (two house) legislature and a supreme court, protection of individual freedoms under a bill of rights, the abolition of slavery, and the establishment of Roman Catholicism as the official religion. Most of the voters in Nicaragua belonged to a political group known as the Liberales. On the opposite side was a group called the Serviles. The Liberales feared that the Serviles, most of whom lived in Guatemala, wanted too much control over the United Provinces.

The first president of the United Provinces was a Liberal named Manuel José Arce. In 1827 a civil war broke out between the two political groups. In 1829 President Arce and the provincial army were able to defeat the rebel forces led by Francisco Morazán, but it was clear that the future of the union was in doubt. In 1830 Morazán was elected president, and he held this office until the break-up of the union in 1838.

Nicaragua led the movement to destroy the union. In 1838 Nicaragua was the first nation to withdraw from the United Provinces. The next few years in Nicaraguan history were stormy ones. At long last the Nicaraguans had their own country, their own light-blue-and-white flag, and their own national anthem. However, the years of tight Spanish control had not prepared Nicaragua very well for freedom. Nicaraguans had to learn how to govern themselves without fighting. This was not an easy task.

Nicaragua Stands Alone

Until the middle of the nineteenth century, Nicaraguans fought viciously among themselves and many people died. They could not agree on a capital city and moved it from León to Masaya before finally settling on Managua in 1858. The central government was weak, and bandits ran freely through the countryside. Besides outlaws, the shaky new government had to worry about interference from stronger, more well-established nations. Chief among these was the United States. Over the years the United States's relationship with Nicaragua, as with other Latin American nations, has been troubled and complex. The United States has been the best friend and protector of many Latin American nations, but the price for that friendship has often been more than the smaller countries bargained for.

The relationship between the United States and Nicaragua began in 1823 when Nicaragua was still a part of the United Provinces. In that year the United States issued the Monroe Doctrine. This document was a warning to the nations of Europe that the United States would not tolerate any further colonization in Latin America. The struggling new nations of Central and South America welcomed this support for their independence. What they did not appreciate, and would learn to regret even more as time went on, was the second part of President James Monroe's statement. He claimed that the United States would not tolerate any further colonization in South America, a policy that led to increased United States intervention in Latin American disputes.

Behind the words of the Monroe Doctrine were fears that have colored U.S. relationships with Central American nations ever since. The United States has worried that revolution or instability in Central America might provide enemies of the United States with a military base in the Western Hemisphere.

The United States
Plans a Canal

Coupled with United States determination to control events in the Western Hemisphere was a much more tangible desire that caused the United States to look specifically at Nicaragua. The United States raced with such nations as France and Great Britain to be the first nation to build a canal across the Central American isthmus. Interest in this canal intensified after the discovery of gold in California in 1849. There were two ways for people living on the East Coast of the United States to reach the California gold fields: by ship around the tip of South America or by horse across the North American continent. Both ways were long and dangerous. A canal across the isthmus would cut the ocean trip by more than half.

Nicaragua seemed to be the ideal location for such a canal. As early as the 1500s the Spanish king, Philip II, had asked his engineer, Batista Antonelli, to draw up plans for a canal. The plans called for a canal from the Pacific to the western shore of Lake Nicaragua. From the lake, boats could then pass to the Caribbean by way of the San Juan River. This same plan was the one people dreamed about for the next three hundred years.

In 1850 the United States and Great Britain, each fearful that the other would negotiate with Nicaragua for the right to build a canal, signed an agreement called the Clayton-Bulwer Treaty. In this treaty both the United States and Great Britain guaranteed that they would never use force in order to build a canal in Nicaragua or in any other part of Central America. Years later, in 1901, the British and the Americans signed a second treaty called the Hay-Pauncefote Treaty. Under the terms of this second treaty, Britain agreed that the United States could build a canal in Central America. The United States decided to build a canal in Panama instead of in Nicaragua, and so for a while it lost interest in Nicaragua.

Even though the U.S. government decided against a canal route through Nicaragua, individual American businessmen did not. Their plans, too, would have an impact on Nicaraguan politics. In the same year that the Clayton-Bulwer Treaty was signed, an American named Cornelius Vanderbilt decided that he would build a passageway across Nicaragua. Instead of a canal, he wanted to connect the Atlantic and the Pacific by a transportation system that combined railways with the waterways of Lake Nicaragua and the San Juan River.

Political Changes from
Walker to Zelaya

Vanderbilt's company attracted other Americans to Nicaragua. Most important of these was a man named William Walker. Walker was an adventurer from California who believed that the United States should expand until it controlled all of Latin America. William Walker had many reasons for going to Nicaragua: he wanted personal wealth and fame, and he wanted to conquer new lands that could be used for the expansion of North American slavery.

Walker entered Nicaragua in 1855. By 1856 he had arranged to have himself elected president. During his short presidency, he introduced slavery, made English the official language of the country, and borrowed money from foreign banks. Walker was supported by the Liberals. His time in Central America was short and was destined to end violently. In 1860 he was shot by a firing squad.

The Liberals who had invited Walker to come to Nicaragua were based in León. They were opposed by the Conservatives who were based in Granada. Much of the history of nineteenth-century Nicaragua can be explained in terms of the power struggle between these two groups. Each one wanted to control the government.

Many Nicaraguans, especially the Conservatives, were upset and angry that the Liberals had invited a foreigner to interfere so directly in their country. A Conservative general, Tomás Martínez, led the opposition to Walker. When Walker was defeated, Martínez became the president. He remained in power until 1867. Only once during Martínez's presidency was there a serious Liberal threat to his control. In 1863 he suppressed the last major civil rebellion of the nineteenth century. From then

*William Walker's brief tenure in Nicaragua is illustrated
in these two nineteenth-century lithographs:
President Walker reviewing troops on the Grand Plaza in
Granada, and his execution by a firing squad in 1860.*

until 1893 the Conservatives were in power. Martínez was followed by Fernando Guzmán (1867–1871), Vicente Cuadra (1871–1875), Pedro Joaquín Chamorro (1875–1879) Joaquín Zavala (1879–1883), Adán Cárdenas (1883–1887), Evarista Carazo (1887–1889), and Roberto Sacasa (1889–1893). The thirty years of peace and stability under these Conservative rulers are known in Nicaraguan history as *los treinta años*.

The governments during these years were criticized for being repressive to the rights of Indians and other minorities. On the other hand, the Conservatives were praised because the economy of Nicaragua developed further than it ever had before. The plantation system was introduced and coffee production was greatly expanded. American industries such as the United Fruit Company were encouraged to invest in Nicaragua. Because the fruit company became so involved in Nicaraguan affairs, it was nicknamed "El Pulpo," or the Octopus. Under the direction of this powerful firm, banana production increased. During these same years railroads were built and gold mines were organized.

Roberto Sacasa, the Conservative who was elected president in 1889, tried to expand the political power of the country by giving government positions to people from León as well as people from the Conservative stronghold of Granada. This plan backfired because the citizens of Granada resented Sacasa's gestures. In the struggle that followed, a Liberal leader, José Santos Zelaya, gained power.

When Zelaya took office in 1893, the Liberals wrote a new constitution. This would become a pattern in Nicaraguan government, one that contributed to the instability of the nation. Too often in Nicaragua, new leaders wrote new laws. When Zelaya tried to arrange his re-election, rather than let the people choose, his former Liberal supporters rose up against him. In an about-face, the Conservatives in Granada, aided by outside forces from

Honduras, helped Zelaya keep his power. Zelaya stayed in office until 1909. He was a tyrannical ruler who punished his enemies harshly. Nevertheless, he continued to make improvements in Nicaragua's economy, at least for the upper classes. He also helped to modernize Managua, the city of his birth.

The end of Zelaya's rule marked the beginning of a new century and a new era in Nicaraguan politics. In the twentieth century Nicaragua's troubled relationship with the United States would become even more tangled.

CHAPTER 5

NICARAGUA ENTERS THE TWENTIETH CENTURY

In the opening years of the twentieth century, Nicaragua attracted more and more attention from the United States. U.S. involvement in the Nicaraguan economy led to greater involvement in the Nicaraguan government. This outside interference meant that the Nicaraguan presidency rarely changed hands through peaceful political means such as voting. Instead, Nicaraguans in the twentieth century increasingly turned to violence as a way of removing unpopular leaders from office. When the United States intervened in Nicaragua, it only wanted to help. Unfortunately, Americans did not always know what was best for their Central American neighbor.

U.S. Intervention
in Nicaragua

By 1901, the United States had determined that Panama, not Nicaragua, would provide the best location for a canal across the Central American isthmus. The major nineteenth-century reason for North American interest in Nicaragua no longer existed. Instead, the United States focused on Nicaragua because of American fears that the dictatorship of José Santos Zelaya was unfriendly to American businessmen with investments in Nicaragua. By 1908, Zelaya had been in office for fifteen years. Under his leadership the wealthy coffee planters, the *cafeteleros*, had experienced new prosperity.

Zelaya's policy favored large plantation owners at the expense of the plantation workers and small Indian farmers. For example, he gave a government bonus of five centavos for each tree on plantations covering more than 5,000 square feet (465 sq m). Along with the new prosperity under Zelaya went tougher import and export laws for foreigners investing in Nicaragua. Zelaya also supported greater independence for Nicaragua in foreign affairs. Greater independence meant less reliance on the United States.

Many of Zelaya's actions ran counter to the policy of the United States at the time. President Theodore Roosevelt in 1904 had strengthened the North American position in Central America. He had added his own words to the Monroe Doctrine. In his statement, usually called the "Roosevelt Corollary," he maintained that the United States was the leading power in all matters pertaining to the Western Hemisphere and that the United States had the right, if necessary, to use its army and navy in helping Latin American countries achieve stable governments. President Roosevelt compared the United States to a "policeman" whose job was to maintain law and order in Latin America.

Soon after Roosevelt issued his famous statement, three events involving Nicaragua led to direct American intervention in the country. First, in 1906, Zelaya attempted to lead Nicaragua into a war against Guatemala, Honduras, and El Salvador. Neither the United States nor Mexico wanted the conflict to take place. A peace conference was called in Washington, D.C. The United

States demanded, and Mexico agreed, that Central American countries must promise not to intervene in each other's lives.

At about the same time, President Zelaya tried to get the governments of Germany and Japan to build a canal across Nicaragua. This canal would have competed with the Panama Canal built by the United States. The U.S. Secretary of State was worried about the possibility of a German or Japanese canal in Central America. These nations were increasing the size of their navies, and he believed that they were dangerous to the United States. (World War I and World War II would prove that he was right.) The United States felt that Nicaragua was endangering the peace of the entire Western Hemisphere and violating the spirit of the Monroe Doctrine by inviting a European and an Asian nation to become involved in such an important project.

Finally, in 1909, Nicaraguans living in the Bluefields region of the country along the Caribbean coast became angry with Zelaya over a new tax that he imposed upon them. Under the leadership of the Conservative governor of Bluefields, Juan Estrada, the citizens of Bluefields revolted against the central government. They wanted to remove Zelaya from office.

The United States, under the direction of the Secretary of State, Philander C. Knox, supported the rebels. By 1909, under mounting pressure from both inside and outside the country, the sixteen-year dictatorship of José Zelaya had come to an end. Once again in Nicaraguan history, outsiders had helped determine what kind of leadership the country was to have. Over the course of the next few years, United States troops would intervene in Nicaragua many, many times.

Conservatives vs. Liberals

The new Conservative president was a man named Adolfo Díaz. Díaz's plan for Nicaragua was to stabilize the economy and to formalize Nicaragua's economic ties with the United States. He was unpopular, however, and in 1912 he was threatened by another rebellion led by the Liberals. The U.S. government believed that Díaz's economic plans were good ones so the United States sent 2,500 Marines to Nicaragua to help President Díaz put down the rebellion. The Marines conducted a new election in Nicaragua, and Díaz won again. Although most of the Marines went home to the United States, at least one hundred of them were left behind to help President Díaz retain his power.

From 1912 until 1933, the relationship between the United States and Nicaragua remained unchanged. Each time the Marines withdrew, there was a rebellion in Nicaragua and whoever was the American president then ordered the Marines to go back in. In each election the United States backed the Conservative Party candidate. Often, Mexico intervened in these elections by supporting the candidate of the Liberal Party. When political power changed hands, there was always rebellion and fighting. By 1928, there were over five thousand U.S. Marines permanently stationed in Nicaragua.

Even in the 1920s many people criticized the United States for its involvement in Nicaragua. These people were particularly critical of the use of American troops to oversee elections in Nicaragua. Supporters of U.S. intervention argued that Nicaraguans had proven that they were unable to hold free elections without resorting to violence. As one Secretary of State pointed out, there had never been an election in Nicaragua where the person already in power lost. For Nicaraguans this taught a simple, but violent, lesson. If they did not like a leader, there was only one way to remove him—by armed rebellion. What the United States hoped to do was to show Nicaraguans that holding elections was a peaceful way of removing leaders who were unpopular. This was the way that the people of the United States and Great Britain had been using for many years.

*A Nicaraguan farmer suspected of
gunrunning is stopped for
questioning by U.S. Marines in 1927.*

The United States did not oversee the elections for bad reasons. They wanted Nicaraguans to have the same kind of government and election process that the United States had because they believed that this form of government, democracy, was best for all nations. From the beginning they were honest in their reasons for wanting this—the Americans believed that a stable, democratic government in Nicaragua, as well as in other Latin American nations, would be in the best interest of the United States as well as their southern neighbors.

Perhaps the United States's biggest mistake was in not realizing that Nicaragua is its own country with its own traditions and customs. The Conservatives and the Liberals were not like the two major U.S. political parties, the Democrats and the Republicans. Whether or not people called themselves Liberals or Conservatives depended on their social standing, their family backgrounds, and their loyalties to the city of León or to the city of Granada. Their political parties had little to do with their political beliefs.

Furthermore, Nicaragua was not a democratic country where all people voted and shared in the government. The people who belonged to the two political parties, the people who voted, and the people who fought over the election results were members of the upper class, or aristocracy. The greatest numbers of people, the workers and the peasant farmers, were not involved in the political process at all. So, when the United States tried to bring democracy to Nicaragua by supporting the Conservative Party, they missed the majority of the people. And, without the support of the majority of the people, there can be no democracy.

By the late 1920s, the United States was beginning to realize that American democracy could not be imposed upon Nicaragua by the U.S. Marines. Rather than try to hold free elections, they decided to compromise. They agreed to support any Nicaraguan leader who could promise the United States two things: peace in Nicaragua and friendship with the United States. It did not matter anymore whether or not this person was a dictator, as long as the leadership met these two conditions.

The Rise of Somoza

In 1927, President Calvin Coolidge sent his Secretary of State, Henry Stimson, to work out this agreement. The Nicaraguans agreed that President Díaz would serve out his term as president and that the Marines would oversee one last election in 1932 and then the Marines would withdraw. Meanwhile the Marines would help train a local National Guard that could be used by the Nicaraguan president to keep the peace after the U.S. troops had left the country.

In 1932, the election was held and a former rebel, the Liberal Juan Bautista Sacasa, won the presidency. True to the American promise, the Marines were withdrawn. Although Sacasa was the elected president, the head of the National Guard, Anastasio Somoza García, emerged as the most powerful man in Nicaragua. In 1934 he electrified the nation by arranging the assassination of the rebel hero, Augusto César Sandino. In 1936, Sacasa resigned as president, and Somoza took over from him on January 1, 1937.

The rise of Somoza to the presidency began a forty-two year family dictatorship. Under the rule of the Somozas, the United States continued to receive the two things it had demanded in the compromise of 1927: political stability and Nicaraguan loyalty to American policies. At the same time, however, the Nicaraguan people lost even the small measure of democracy that they had enjoyed under Marine supervision. The Somozas were absolute dictators. Although they pretended to hold elections according to the Nicaraguan constitution, the only people who won were the people they wanted to win. When presidents did not follow the orders of the Somoza family, they were quickly removed from office. For example, in the 1940s President Leonardo Argüello tried to reform the government against the wishes of the Somozas. His presidency lasted one month.

Although the Somozas allowed some people outside the family to hold the position of president, they never allowed anyone but a family member to control the National Guard. The Guard provided the police force that kept the family in power. Nicaraguans came to fear and respect the National Guard. In each region the National Guardsmen had control over local politics. People who wanted special requests from the government had to be in good favor with their local branch of the Guards.

The reign of the Somozas was not always peaceful, but even in the worst of times, they managed to retain control of Nicaragua. There were attempts at rebellion in 1954, 1959, and 1967, all of which were suppressed by the Guards. In 1956 Anastasio Somoza was assassinated by a poet, Rigoberto López Pérez. Somoza was immediately succeeded by his son, Luis. Luis relinquished the presidency in 1963 to a Somoza family "puppet." ("Puppet" is the term used to describe a leader who is controlled by someone who is not officially a member of the government.) This "puppet" president, René Schick Gutiérrez, was a tolerant leader as dictators go. In 1967 he died and was replaced by Anastasio Somoza's second son, Anastasio, Jr.

Except for a few months in 1972, Anastasio, Jr., known as Tachito, controlled Nicaragua until the revolution of 1979 brought an end to the rule of the Somozas. Throughout his years in office the conditions that led to the revolution were building. The wealthy agricultural landowners became wealthier, and the peasants became poorer. Civil liberties such as freedom of the press, freedom of speech, and the right to vote were taken away. The mass of the people did not share in the industrial development of the nation.

Tachito Somoza might have been able to ignore these conditions as so many Nicaraguan dictators had before him. He continued to enjoy the reluctant support of American presidents. However, two forces were operating in Nicaragua that were beyond his control. One was the devastating earthquake that destroyed much of Managua in 1972. The second was the spirit of rebellion that was coursing through Latin American countries. Dictatorships all over the area were threatened by people's rebellions. The rebel forces had the successful example of Castro's Cuba to give them hope.

*Marking the end of a forty-two year dynasty,
President Anastasio Somoza held a press conference
in Managua on July 16, 1979, to announce his
resignation. Samoza then left for exile in Miami,
and three days later Sandinista rebel forces
marched triumphantly into the capital city.*

CHAPTER 6

REVOLUTION

On July 19, 1979, President Anastasio Somoza left Nicaragua to live in exile in Miami, Florida. After forty-two years the Somoza family dictatorship had ended. Rebel forces, calling themselves the Sandinistas, had taken over the government.

At first it was hard to tell who or what the Sandinistas stood for. Although their leaders claimed that they had no ties with any one special group outside Nicaragua, many people—especially in the United States—believed they were Communists. However, although the Sandinistas received aid from the Communist government in Cuba, they also had close relations with Mexico, a non-Communist country. One thing was certain: the Sandinistas opposed Somoza. Their coalition government was made up of anti-Somoza people who had been kept out of power for years. The new government included people of wealth, as long as those people opposed Somoza. The era of Somoza had ended, and the Sandinistas promised change for the government of Nicaragua.

Nicaragua's revolution of 1979 followed a pattern of rebellion that had been spreading throughout the world since the end of World War II. Since 1945 many people in small nations throughout the world had struggled for their independence against colonial powers and local dictatorships. In the 1950s, many Latin American nations had overthrown dictatorships. Powerful men such as Juan Péron in Argentina, Pérez Jiménez in Venezuela, Rojas Pinilla in Colombia and Rafael Trujillo in the Dominican Republic were all overthrown or assassinated.

The fall of any dictator attracted attention, of course, but the biggest headlines in newspapers around the world had come with the news of the revolution in Cuba in 1959. A rebel leader, Fidel Castro, had toppled the government of the dictator Fulgencio Batista. Castro had rallied the people of Cuba behind him, and he was a Communist with good friends in the government of the Soviet Union.

Unlike other violent changes in the government of Latin American countries, the revolution in Cuba meant a real change in power and policy. The Cuban government had not just changed from one group of wealthy landowners to another group of wealthy landowners. Instead power had passed to people who had never had power before.

The revolution in Nicaragua followed the model of the Cuban revolution. Like Castro's rebellion, it had been planned for a long time. When the Sandinistas were finally able to topple Somoza, they knew they had the support of thousands of Nicaraguans from all classes who could no longer tolerate the way in which the Somozas were running their country.

Augusto César Sandino

Rebel groups were not new to Nicaragua. In fact, the Sandinistas took their name from a man who had led a rebel movement against Anastasio Somoza, Sr., back in the 1930s. This man was Augusto César Sandino. Sandino's story is important in understanding the background of the most recent Nicaraguan revolution.

Sandino was born in Nicaragua in 1898. His father was a wealthy plantation owner and his mother was an Indian who worked on his father's estate. Because his mother was an Indian, Sandino was never accepted by the wealthy society who were his father's friends. Sandino grew up knowing that there were many Nicaraguans, among them Indians like his mother, who did not have a fair share of the nation's wealth.

As a young man Sandino traveled throughout Latin America, living first in Guatemala and then in Mexico. Everywhere he went he found many poor people and a few very rich people. He learned that most of the wealthy people who were in power were supported by the United States government. For this reason he came to believe that life in his country of Nicaragua would be better for poor citizens if Nicaraguans could remove the United States Marines from the country.

In 1926 Sandino raised a small army of rebels to fight against the government of Díaz, which, as we learned in the last chapter, was supported by the United States. Sandino's fighters carried a red-and-black flag. Their motto was *Patria libre o morir*. In English this means "A free country or death."

Sandino and his supporters did not want to compromise. Even when the Conservative Party reached an agreement with the Liberal Party in the late 1920s, Sandino would not stop fighting. Like Castro in Cuba many years later, Sandino did not believe that compromises between the old political parties went far enough. He believed that these were deals made by wealthy men and that these agreements would not really change the lives of Indians and peasant workers.

Finally in 1932, when the United States agreed to withdraw

the Marines from Nicaragua, Sandino agreed to stop fighting. He moved to a farm near Rio Cao where he hoped to develop a new model of farming. Sandino believed that Nicaraguans who had never owned land before should band together on large co-operative farms that they would own together. He did not think they should continue to work for the large, wealthy landowners who paid such low wages. If peasants owned their own farms together, he believed, they would eventually control the economy and the government of Nicaragua.

By 1934, Anastasio Somoza was head of the National Guard and was fast becoming the most powerful man in Nicaragua. He disagreed with Sandino. In fact he thought Sandino's plans would destroy the economy of Nicaragua. On February 21, 1934, Somoza arranged for Sandino to come to Managua. When Sandino arrived, he was assassinated.

By arranging the death of Sandino, Somoza removed a potential enemy. However, the people of Nicaragua lost a hero they had loved and admired very much. They kept the spirit of Sandino alive, and they vowed that some day the Somoza family would pay for Sandino's death even if it took many years.

Nicaragua under Somoza

Meanwhile, the Somozas grew rich. Throughout the 1930s, forties, and fifties, they expanded their control of the Nicaraguan economy. They began by taking over much of the cattle

Augusto Sandino, the Nicaraguan patriot and folk hero, was assassinated at the command of the senior Somoza in 1934.

raising, coffee growing, and gold mining of Nicaragua. In the 1950s, the family moved into new areas—textile manufacturing, tobacco production, food processing, and transportation. By the time Anastasio Somoza, Jr., was forced to flee the country, the Somozas owned 7,722 square miles (about 20,000 square km) of land in Nicaragua, and each member of the family was a multimillionaire.

The people who opposed the Somozas watched angrily as the wealth of the family grew over the years. What angered them most was that so few people in Nicaragua had so much while all the rest of the people were poor. By only allowing his family and friends to have power in the government and in business, Somoza increased the wealth of the rich while the poor got poorer and poorer.

He did not like to spend money on things like health care, water purification, or schooling. Because of this, by 1970 only 2 percent of the workers in agricultural regions had good drinking water, and only 25 percent of the people living in Managua had sewage facilities. Fewer than half of all Nicaraguans could read and write, so it was hard for them to get better jobs. There were very few doctors in the country, and those who were available were so expensive that only rich people could afford to see them.

By 1970, fewer than 25 percent of all the landowners in Nicaragua owned over 80 percent of the land. This means that very few people controlled most of the country. Over half of the people had an average yearly income of only $250. Meanwhile, the wealthy landowners were buying more and more land. Peasants who had lived on small farms for many generations were forced off their land and had no choice but to go live in terrible poverty in the *barrios* (slums) of cities like Managua and Masaya.

The Roots of Rebellion

Although conditions had been bad for many years, the Somozas did nothing to help the plight of the poor. As the few wealthy families grew richer and richer with Somoza's support, the poor people became more desperate as they searched for ways to feed and house their families. Besides the worsening economic situation, two forces came together in the 1970s that helped stimulate revolution. First, all through the 1960s, a small group of people loyal to the memory of Sandino had been watching the changes Castro had been making in Cuban society. In Cuba, too, a small group of wealthy people had controlled the country until Castro's rebellion, and as part of his government he forced the wealthy to share their large plantations with their former workers.

This was Communism, however, and many Nicaraguans believed in capitalism and democracy. They did not want to force anyone, even wealthy plantation owners, to give up their land against their will. They wanted the wealthy to share the responsibility for the poor by paying more taxes that would support schools, hospitals, sanitation projects, and roads in poor areas. They knew Somoza would not tax himself or his wealthy friends, so they wanted free elections to remove the dictator and to install a fairer kind of government.

It took the second big event to get these people to join with the Communist group. This event was the earthquake of 1972 that caused many deaths and destroyed much of Managua. The United States and the United Nations sent millions of dollars to help the Nicaraguans in this crisis. The Somozas used much of this money to rebuild and expand their own businesses while the economy of Nicaragua grew weaker and weaker. This gave all the groups opposed to Somoza a reason to unite to overthrow his dictatorship.

Between the earthquake in 1972 and the resignation of Somoza in 1979, Nicaragua was a nation in a state of civil war. That meant that Nicaraguans were fighting against Nicaraguans. The people who supported Somoza were the members of the National Guard and the wealthiest business owners and large farmers. The people who opposed Somoza came from many groups, but together made up an organization called the Frente Sandinista de Liberacíon Nacional, made up of middle-class opponents of Somoza; several radical Communist groups; and the military Insurrectionists, led by the national hero, Edén Pastora Gómez, popularly known as Commander Zero.

The FSLN tried to get Somoza to leave the country peacefully. They wanted him to hold new elections and allow anyone who wanted to run for president. They wanted him to use government money to improve conditions for all Nicaraguans.

When he refused, the FSLN began the war. There was fighting throughout the countryside and in the barrios of the cities. Somoza's National Guard fought back and even bombed areas of Nicaragua where rebels were believed to be the strongest. By 1978, Somoza had to leave Managua when Commander Zero and his troops captured the National Palace. In August and September of 1978 the rebel forces gained new power. They attacked the government troops in Managua, León, Estelí, Chincurdega, and Masaya.

Many of the Sandinista rebels were very young men and women who believed that their only hope for a better future was the overthrow of Somoza. These young rebels were nicknamed *Los Muchachos*, Spanish for the children. When Somoza finally resigned in July 1979, there was much rejoicing among the Sandinista forces. However, their leaders knew that the fight had just begun.

President Somoza with National Guard troops in June 1979

*A Sandinista batallion patrols the countryside.
The Sandinista program for economic reform
has been stalled by the ongoing civil war.*

Problems for the
Sandinista Regime

There were two problems that the new leaders faced in 1979 and would continue to face for some time. First, they had to organize a government that would continue to have the support of most Nicaraguans. Second, they had to continue fighting against small but well-armed forces who remained loyal to Somoza.

The Sandinistas first decided to attack problems such as illiteracy, poor health care, bad housing conditions, and unemployment. They said that they would hold an election for a new president in 1984, but until then a junta (a group of leaders) would control the country. To many people this seemed like the old dictatorship under a new name. They wanted free elections right away. For this reason several important people who had supported the Sandinistas during the war dropped out of the new government soon after.

The Sandinistas did keep their promises about creating better conditions for the poor in the cities and in the countryside, but without the support of the business owners and large farmers, it has been difficult to make real improvements in the economy. There has been progress, however, in some areas.

The most remarkable change has occurred as a result of the campaign against illiteracy. The Sandinistas believe that the best way to have lots of people participating in government is to teach everyone to read and write. In 1980 the Sandinista Minister of Education received a United Nations prize for his work in reducing the illiteracy rate in Nicaragua. Over 100,000 volunteers of all ages were sent throughout the country to teach people to read and write. Nicknamed the "Crusade of Love," this program reduced illiteracy from well over 50 percent to less than 20 percent in a very short time.

The Sandinistas have also encouraged hundreds of volunteer community workers (called *brigadistas*) to help vaccinate children against polio and measles. Other reforms have been small, but important to the people they have benefited. For example, washerwomen in Nicaraguan hospitals have long been used to cleaning linens over open fires. The Sandinistas have built tin roofs to protect these women from the hot sun. In the barrios, garbage collection and street cleaning are part of daily life for the first time.

The United States and the Sandinistas

In spite of the gains that the Sandinistas have made, they face stiff opposition from the United States and from Nicaraguan guerrillas who receive money and weapons from the United States. These people do not think that the Sandinistas have kept their promises. They are continuing the same kind of warfare that the Sandinistas used to overthrow Somoza. For this reason the opponents to the Sandinistas are called *contras*, a term that is shorthand for counter-revolutionary. Among the contras are Commander Zero, the former Sandinista hero, and many hundreds of Miskito Indians. The Sandinistas forced many of these Indians to leave their homes as part of a land reorganization

Top: *New recruits at a* contra *command center near the Honduran border.* Bottom: *former Sandinista Eden Pastora, popularly known as Commander Zero, is now a* contra *leader.*

plan, and the Indians will not forgive them. The largest group of contras, however, is the Nicaraguan Democratic Force (FDN). This group has strong emotional and financial support from American conservatives.

In November 1984, the Sandinistas held the election that they had promised the country. The leader of the junta, Daniel Ortega, was elected president by about a two-thirds majority. In addition, sixty-one of the ninety-six seats in the National Assembly were won by Sandinistas. The opposition was splintered among many small groups. Many people, including President Ronald Reagan of the United States, believe that the election was unfair. Reagan, like earlier U.S. presidents, is very worried about Communist governments in Latin America. He is very concerned about the close ties between Nicaragua and Cuba.

In addition, Reagan and other Americans are angered by the Sandinistas' censorship of free press. Under the Somozas, newspapers hostile to the dictator were allowed to publish their views because so few of the people could read. With the success of the literacy campaign, many more people can read. The Sandinistas have come to realize the pressure that an open press can put on a country's government when the people are free to read criticism of their leaders.

Many Americans also condemn the Sandinistas' violation of the rights of Indians, and their continued military build-up. Under Somoza, the Nicaraguan army never numbered more than eleven thousand. Under the Sandinistas there are over fifty thousand people in the armed services.

The Sandinistas believe that Nicaragua's friendship with Cuba should not concern the United States. Ortega and the members of his government maintain that they are hampered in their work by the involvement of the United States in their internal affairs. They argue that the contras' illegal raids are the reason they have to impose such strict rules on the freedoms of Nicaraguan citizens.

Embargo

In 1985, President Reagan asked Congress to provide $14 million in aid to the contras. He believes that as many as fifteen thousand contras, many living in refugee camps in Honduras, are ready to take the government of Nicaragua away from the Sandinistas. The contras are publicly pledged to provide Nicaragua with a democratic government friendly to the United States. Because President Reagan is anxious to reduce the influence of Communism in Central America, he is willing to aid the contras.

Congress, however, did not want to risk a war in Central America. They voted against the aid plan. As another way of opposing the Sandinistas, President Reagan ordered an embargo against Nicaragua in May 1985. This order prohibits any direct trade between Nicaragua and the United States.

Furthermore, Nicaraguan planes and ships are forbidden to enter the United States. There is much disagreement about the effectiveness of such an embargo. People sympathetic to the Sandinistas believe that economic pressure will force the government to seek aid from Communist countries. In the weeks immediately following the embargo, President Ortega received promises from many Communist nations—including Russia, Cuba, and Bulgaria—that they would help fill in the trade gaps left by the departure of the U.S. from Nicaraguan markets.

Nicaraguans face many challenges as they look to the future. As in the past there is much disagreement among them about how best to meet these challenges. One thing is certain. Regardless of their political views, all Nicaraguans hope for a better, more peaceful, richer future for their country.

CHAPTER 7

A LAND OF
ENDURING
TRADITIONS

No matter what government is in power in Nicaragua, there are certain customs and habits of the Nicaraguan people that remain the same. In the four hundred years since the Spaniards first began living with the native Indian peoples of Nicaragua, many traditions have been established that help define what being a Nicaraguan is all about.

A Mixed Religious Heritage:
Roman Catholicism
and Indian Spiritualism

Almost everyone in Nicaragua is a member of the Roman Catholic Church, and religious holidays are times of great celebration. Not only do Nicaraguans like to celebrate traditional church holidays like Christmas and Easter, but each town or city has a patron saint whose special day is a reason for feasts and parades. In many places the traditions of the Indians have been added to the religious customs of the Catholic Church. Historians believe that the Indians adapted so readily to Christianity because the Nicarao symbol for their God of Rain was very similar to the Christian cross. Even Indians who have converted to Christianity preserve some of their traditional practices. For example, many Indians still worship their ancestors through shamans who go into trances to receive messages from people who have died.

In many areas Indian traditions are carried out through dance and music. In Granada each year a celebration called "The Dance of the Little Devils" combines both Indian and Spanish styles of music. In Masaya the annual fiesta honoring Saint Jeronimo, the patron saint of that city, is a time for Indians to display their handicrafts. The same is true for Diriamba's festival of Saint Sebastian. In the capital city, August 1 is always a day of great festivity because it is the feast day of Managua's patron saint, Domingo.

Sports

As strong as the influence of Spain has been on the development of Nicaraguan customs and pastimes, there is one area in which the United States has had a greater influence than Spain. This is baseball. No Nicaraguan celebration is complete without a baseball game. In most Latin American countries, as in Spain, the most popular sports are bullfighting and soccer. But this is not true in Nicaragua. Here the national sport is baseball. Almost everyone likes to play and people follow their favorite teams in their struggle to become national champion.

The Heritage of the People

The traditions of Nicaragua are a blend of many cultures, and so are the people. Almost 70 percent of the people call themselves mestizos. This means that they have a mix of Spanish and Indian ancestors. Only about 5 percent of the people are pure Indian and another 15 percent or so are pure Caucasian. Fewer than 10 percent of the people are pure black and 2 or 3 percent are known as Zambos, a mix of black and Indian. A group of Nicaraguans with a particularly interesting heritage are the Black Caribs. These people live in the Pearl Lagoon region. They are English-speaking people who were taken as slaves by early British settlers to the British West Indies. The Black Caribs later migrated or were taken as slaves to the British colony on the Miskito coast. They remained there after slavery was abolished in 1824.

Daily Life and Customs

Because Nicaragua is a tropical country, almost everyone dresses casually most of the time in light, cool, cotton clothing. The most colorful dress is reserved for carnivals and fiestas. Nicaraguans of all types dress alike, and, for the most part, they share a common diet. Maize and cacao are still staple foods as they have been for many generations. The most common foods are tortillas, tamales, atoles, rice, and beans. Nicaraguans like to drink a chocolate beverage made of ground cacao and maize. This popular drink is kept cool and is often served in wooden gourds.

People in Nicaragua tend to stay in the same towns where their ancestors have lived for generations. It is not uncommon to find hundreds of people in the same small town who share the same last name. Relatives are extremely important, and people do not like to move too far from their families. To outsiders, Nicaraguan names can be confusing. Men put their mother's family name at the end of their names. For example, President

Somoza's full name was Anastasio Somoza García, and the new president's full name is Daniel Ortega Saavedra. Daniel is his first name, Ortega is his father's family (or last) name, and Saavedra was his mother's last name before she married. He is referred to as Señor or President Ortega. A woman's name is different. If she marries, she is most likely to drop her mother's name and add her husband's name with the small word "de" in front of it. For example, if a girl named Luisa Garcia Ortega married a man named José Rafael Martínez, she would become Luisa Garcia de Rafael.

The average Nicaraguan woman gets married at the age of fourteen, and the average Nicaraguan man gets married at age fifteen. (Perhaps because of this young marriage age, anyone sixteen or over can vote.) Women in Nicaragua can expect to live until the age of fifty-seven, and men in Nicaragua can expect to live until the age of fifty-four. Until very recently over half of the people who died each year in Nicaragua were children under five years of age.

Perhaps because of this high rate of infant death, families in Nicaragua tend to be large. The average family has six children. All children must attend primary school, but after that they may go to work rather than go on to high school. About half of all Nicaraguans aged twelve to seventeen attend school. Because of the climate schools are in session from May through September, the rainy season.

Farming and Business

Another reason for schoolchildren to have a vacation during the dry season is that most Nicaraguan children live in agricultural areas and are needed to help with farm work. Although industry has grown rapidly since World War II, Nicaragua is

Top: *A worker in a cotton cooperative outside Leon*
Bottom: *A man harvests coffee beans with a rifle strapped to his back, a bleak commentary on life in Nicaragua today.*

still a predominantly agricultural country. Almost half of all the people who are employed in Nicaragua work on farms. The most important crops are coffee, cotton, rice, bananas, corn, beans, cocoa, and tobacco. The size of Nicaraguan farms is measured in *manzanas*. Each manzana equals about one and three-quarters acres. There are about 2.1 million acres (1,200,-000 manzanas) of arable (able to be farmed) land in Nicaragua. Of the 1.2 million acres (685,714 manzanas) that are actively cultivated, 780,000 (445,714 manzanas) of them are planted in cotton and rice. Another large area of farmland is used for grazing animals that are then used for their meat and dairy products.

Agriculture has expanded greatly in recent years; the increase in cotton production in the 1950s and 1960s meant that the value of agricultural products multiplied many times during those years. Much of the coffee, cotton, and sugar that the Nicaraguans grow is exported to other countries. This is very important for their economy, because in exchange for these farm products, the Nicaraguans can import things they need such as machinery, cars, and chemicals.

Even though industry in Nicaragua has historically been less important to the economy than agriculture, industrial products are growing in value. Leading industries include sugar processing, the production of cooking oil, cement manufacturing, food processing, and the manufacture of leather goods. Mining is still important. The chief metals from Nicaraguan mines are tungsten, silver, gold, and copper. Two other important sources of wealth for Nicaragua are lumber and fish. The seafood is particularly rich along the Caribbean where lobsters and varieties of ocean fish are part of the annual haul. In the 1980s, the average yearly catch of fish has been close to 9,500 tons (about 9,000 metric tons). In the highland areas lumber companies harvest fine woods such as mahogany, ebony, and rosewood.

Over the years Nicaragua's most important trading partners have been the United States, Venezuela, West Germany, Japan, Costa Rica, and Guatemala. The Nicaraguan unit of money is called a *córdoba*, after the early explorer. Each *córdoba* is equal to one hundred centavos. Usually, a córdoba is equal to about ten cents in United States money.

The Structure of Government

Nicaragua is not divided into states or provinces. Instead the country is organized into sixteen departments. The largest of these departments has the same name as the largest city in Nicaragua. It is Managua. In terms of population, the smallest department is Rio San Juan. The other departments are Boaco, Carazo, Chinandega, Chontales, Estelí, Granada, Jinotega, León, Madriz, Masaya, Matagalpa, Nueva Segovia, Rivas, and Zelaya.

Under the terms of the latest constitution, there are ninety elected representatives in the National Assembly. Each department is assigned a certain number of representatives according to population. People in all departments vote directly for president and vice-president. The courts are also spread throughout the country, with each court district representing several departments. The Supreme Court of Justice sits in Managua. The next most important courts are called "the chambers of second instance." They are located in five sites—León, Masaya, Granada, Matagalpa and Bluefields.

The president of Nicaragua has a group of advisers called ministers. They are each responsible for a different area of the government. For example, there are ministers of culture, foreign affairs, and social welfare. Many Roman Catholic priests serve in these government positions. The hierarchy of the Church does not approve of this mixing of religion and government, however, and priests like Miguel d'Escoto Brockman, Ernesto Cardenal, and Edgard Parredes may have to decide whether they will be priests or government leaders. In addition to this cabinet of ministers, Nicaragua under the Sandinistas has had a Council of State that includes representatives from a variety of political parties, labor unions, and business associations.

Women in Nicaragua

As is true of women in other Latin American countries, Nicaraguan women have long been considered second-class citizens. They have had many fewer rights and economic opportunities than have Nicaraguan men. Today, however, women are playing an increasingly important role in government. Nicaraguan women have been permitted to vote only since 1955, but more and more of them hold government positions. One important Nicaraguan is Lea Guido de López who serves as the Minister of Health and in 1982 was named the first woman president of the Pan American Health Organization. Nevertheless, there are still many laws that discriminate against women. At public rallies banners saying, *Leyes que perjudiquen a las mujeres . . . Abolicion*, are a familiar sight. This slogan means, "Abolish laws that discriminate against women." Slowly the Sandinistas are responding to the demands of Nicaraguan women. They are aware that their success in the revolution depended on the hundreds of women who fought in the Sandinista forces.

Art and Literature

It may seem that all Nicaraguans are soldiers, farmers, or politicians. However, this is not so. Many Nicaraguans have been poets, artists, and writers. In fact, one of the most famous Latin

American poets was a Nicaraguan. His name was Rubén Darío. Darío was born in 1867. The town where he was born was renamed Ciudad Darío in his honor. In addition, the highest national prize for poetry is named for him. In Darío's poetry, art and spiritual values are associated with Latin America, and materialism and false values are associated with North America. Among Darío's most famous works are *Azul (Blue), Prosas Profanas (Profane Prose)*, and *Cantos de Vida y Esperanza (Songs of Life and Hope)*. Although Darío is probably Nicaragua's most famous poet, the country has claimed many others. They include Marío Sánchez, Joaquín Pasos, and Santiago Arguëllo. Nicaragua can also boast that it is the birthplace of the famous Latin American novelist, Hernán Robleto. He wrote the novel *Sangre en el Tropico (Blood in the Tropics.)*

Nicaragua has also produced many artists. Among them are the famous sculptor, Genaro Amador Lira, and the painter, Asilia Guillén, whose most famous paintings capture the beauty of Las Isletas, the volcanic islands dotting Lake Nicaragua. Omar de León, César Caracas, and Jaime Villa are other Nicaraguans who have made international reputations for their art work. In the field of music Nicaragua's most famous composer is Luis A. Delgadillo.

In its literature, in its art, in its government, in its customs, and in its culture, Nicaragua is a nation with traditions and habits that are uniquely its own. Nicaraguans are proud of the blue-and-white flag that symbolizes their nation. Spanish, Indians, mestizos, or Black Caribs, they share an identity as Nicaraguans.

However, Nicaraguans also share a history of violence, totalitarian government, intolerance, and weak economic systems. Poverty, disease, illiteracy, infant mortality, racial injustice, and repression continue to plague the tiny Central American nation. It will take all Nicaraguans working together to make a better future for their country.

INDEX